THROUGH MARY'S EYES

*Reflections
of Her
Life and Times*

FRANCIS CORDIS BERNARDO, S.C.

*PAULIST PRESS
New York / Mahwah, N.J.*

Cover design by James F. Brisson

Cover illustration by Sister Mary Grace, O.P.

Interior illustrations by Sister Mary Culhane, S.C.

Interior design by Kathleen Doyle

Library of Congress Cataloging-in-Publication Data

Bernardo, Francis Cordis, 1939–
    Through Mary's eyes : reflections of her life and times / Francis Cordis Bernardo.
        p.   cm.
    ISBN 0-8091-3745-3 (alk. paper)
    1. Mary, Blessed Virgin, Saint—Meditations. I. Title.
BT608.5.B47   1997
232.91—dc21   97-25008
                                                       CIP

Published by Paulist Press
997 Macarthur Boulevard
Mahwah, New Jersey 07430

Printed and bound in the
United States of America

Contents

Dedication

*To all women who have allowed the Spirit to
work in them
and through them—
especially Mom and Helen Cratty, S.C.*

Acknowledgments

*To: Ellen Cise Mejias for all her hours
of typing and computer skills.*

*To: Sr. Marie Harold Grady, S.C.,
for her editing skills.*

*To: Author Ann Johnson for her
careful reading of the text
and for sharing the benefits
of her breadth of knowledge.*

*To: All who encouraged me
with their support and love.*

Introduction

I offer these reflections as a meditation, as a prayerful insight into the meeting of the human and divine. Their "diary" format is an attempt to uncover Mary's thoughts, emotions, fears, joys, remembrances, her full human journey and radical openness to the presence of God: Mary, mother, wife, woman.

It is this openness that not only speaks of Mary's fiat, but allows her words, "I am the handmaid of the Lord," to become a reality, a witness of the presence of God. Mary's fears are our fears; Mary's questions are our questions; Mary's sorrows are our sorrows; Mary's joys are our joys. She invites us to journey with her and, in so doing, to open ourselves to the fullness of life as we speak our "Yes!"

A TIME OF
BEGINNING

THE ANNUNCIATION
Luke 1:26 –38

The heavens are filled with more stars than one can count this evening. The gentle breeze comes as a refreshment and brings soothing relief.

The events of this day seem as a dream and yet my being is filled with the heavenly rays that dot the sky.

The messenger called me blessed. Can I, a simple Jewish girl, find such favor with God?

The stories of Yahweh's favor and of the promised savior have been proclaimed throughout my people's history. Abraham and Sarah, Moses and Myriam, the prophets Isaiah and Jeremiah, King David, have all declared a time of deliverance. Mama and papa have given voice to our religious traditions. Long have we waited for the promise to be fulfilled.

Did I imagine all of this? How can it be? I am filled with a surge of energy, the source of which is God, Yahweh.

It is confusing to me. I do not fully understand. How do I tell my parents? What of Joseph? Will he understand?

Yet the stars speak to me of a hope of things to be, of possibilities and dreams fulfilled. As they dance

4

in the sky, I can envision angels dancing before the throne of God with expectant joy, the very joy that fills my soul.

Fiat! I open myself to you, Yahweh. I trust completely. I rest and sleep in your arms tonight.

Reflection

Amid confusion and questioning, Mary remains faithful to Yahweh's call. How does Mary's openness to Yahweh speak to you?

THE VISITATION
Luke 1:39 –56

Tomorrow I set out through the hill country to be with Elizabeth. Our ages have not separated us for she has been my confidante, my mentor, my friend. Her faithfulness and trust in Yahweh have now been blessed. How my joy is increased that Elizabeth and I carry life within us and are able to praise God together! She shares my joy, but she will also understand my confusion and awe my questioning.

What can all of this mean? What lies before us? What will be asked of the children within our wombs? Elizabeth must be feeling some of the same emotions, doubts, fears. I can hardly wait to embrace her.

The journey took longer than I expected. How often I had run across the fields and skipped along the hillside! This time my steps were slower. I needed to stop and rest, marking each mile and bend in the road. The child within me kicked and stirred for want of rest. As I caught sight of the house, my excitement increased.

How radiant Elizabeth looked, how filled with joy! Her advanced years laughed at the wonder and marvels God wrought in her life.

As we embraced each other, the babies within us

danced, and the presence of the most high overshadowed us, and his promise was fulfilled.

Today I return to Nazareth. My time here has come to an end and I must be about the Lord's work. It was good for me to have been here. Elizabeth needed help, my companionship, and I needed to experience again her care, her love, her friendship, her wisdom.

We are one now. We take delight in the trust Yahweh has placed in us. As she nears the time of her delivery, I anticipate the birth of my own child and wonder about the destiny of each child. Her trust gives me strength; her faithfulness, courage. I am at peace. I shall miss her.

Reflection

Elizabeth and Mary bonded together to find strength. Who are the persons in your life who give you strength? Thank God for them.

THE BETROTHAL
Matthew 1:18–24

Although I have seen Joseph daily during our betrothal, I have been unable to bring myself to tell him my fears. How do I begin to tell him all that has taken place, all that is in my heart?

It will soon become apparent, however, that I am with child. What will he think? He is a good and gentle man, upright and just, God-fearing and faithful to our ancestors. I will be a cause of embarrassment to him. Perhaps Joseph will choose to write a letter of divorce.

I cannot bear to hurt him, yet I am asking him for complete trust.

Before Joseph spoke any words, I saw in his eyes that he had said yes, that he had accepted the Lord working in and through him. Then his words gave witness. "I do not understand how the spirit has brought this about. I do not know completely what lies ahead, or what it is that Yahweh is asking of me. Yet you shall come into my house. You shall be my wife and I shall father this child. When the time arrives, we shall name him Emmanuel, for God will be in our midst."

Reflection

Joseph didn't have all the answers to the questions put before him. The angel had declared that the birth of the child was of the spirit, but all the pieces that lay ahead were not in place. Joseph, like Mary, needed to proclaim his "yes."

Think of times in your own life when answers have been difficult in coming, when doubt and confusion existed. How does Mary and Joseph's "yes" speak to you? What is the "yes" you need to say?

ANNOUNCEMENT OF CENSUS
Luke 2:1–5

The news of the census has caused much confusion and preoccupation. The village has been turned upside down. Everyone is preparing, packing, and making the necessary arrangements.

Joseph, being of the house of David, has been told that we must go to Bethlehem in order to be registered.

The trip will be long, the roads treacherous, and the hills are overrun with robbers and bandits.

My time of delivery is nearing and I see Joseph's worried look concerning the journey to Bethlehem. This gentle, caring man wants so much to provide for my needs.

I can feel the child within me stirring, kicking, letting me know in so many ways that the appointed time is near. What if the pains begin? If the birth occurs while we are traveling, how shall we provide? Who will be there to assist? We can only pack the most essential items. What shall I take? What shall I leave behind? The cradle Joseph so lovingly carved must surely be left. There is only so much room on the donkey.

What of the weather? The blankets and swaddling clothes will provide some warmth.

Must my child come into the world amid strangers?

Still the words of the angel ring in my ears: "Do not be afraid, the power of the most high will overshadow you. The child to be born will be called the Son of God."

Tomorrow we leave for Bethlehem.

Reflection

Think of a time in your life when circumstances seemed to be uncertain. How does Mary's confidence in Yahweh's promise speak to the events in your life? Where do you place your confidence?

THE ARRIVAL IN BETHLEHEM
Luke 2:1–5 (continued)

The journey was long and tiresome. The crowds on the roads made traveling burdensome and at times fearful. Yet the knowledge that so many are traveling like us, Joseph and me, to the lands of our ancestors draws and binds us together.

We passed old and young, whole families, some traveling on foot, their sacks of provisions on their backs; others, on donkey, or part of a large caravan.

We saw so many faces: some weathered with age, some exchanging a knowing smile as they see that I am with child, others never raising their eyes.

Where will this journey lead us? What will we find in Bethlehem? The Roman legionnaires will occupy all the rooms in the inns. Where will we rest?

It is cold and damp. The pains are coming more frequently. I am frightened that we will not arrive on time. We have searched endlessly, up one street and down another, looking for a suitable area.

Joseph's gentle hand gives me comfort, but I need to find you, Yahweh. I need to feel your presence, hear your voice.

There is something different about this journey:
a sense of excitement, of wonder, a sense of
promise, of new possibilities.

You are present in the dark, cold night and I
proclaim your greatness.

Reflection

*Who are the faces you have met on your life journey?
What is different about your journey now? What
possibilities await you? To whom do you look for
comfort?*

THE INCARNATION
Luke 2:6–7

What joy fills my heart! I praise you, Yahweh, for your love to us. Your promise is fulfilled. I hold in my arms my new-born.

Joseph placed the child in my arms and I gently wrapped him in swaddling clothes. This good, kind, and noble man, who lies beside me, is such a blessing. His pain and sorrow at finding this place, which houses feed for animals and barely offers protection from the cold night air, is troublesome to him. His eyes speak of anguish and despair. He is distraught. But the mystery that embraces us, and the presence of this fragile child, bring exultation and surround us with your peace.

I look into the eyes of my child. He lies so still. He is so innocent, so pure. I wonder, Lord, what the future holds for my child. I fear for him. I want so much to protect him, to keep him close to me.

Yet I know the Lord's spirit rests upon him, this child of mine. I know he is the promised one.

I seek your strength as Joseph and I strive to attend to the needs of our new-born son.

Reflection

What do you need to ask of the Lord? How does the Lord's spirit rest upon you? Where is the spirit leading you?

THE SHEPHERDS
Luke 2:15–20

The night is still. The stars light up the sky and the moon brightly shines.

Joseph, exhausted, sleeps. He lies beside me. His soft breathing is quiet and restful.

I nestle my child and sing a lullaby mama sang to me. All the waiting, the anticipation has ended; and I am calm and peaceful.

Joseph stirs and opens his eyes. He reaches toward me. We embrace and watch the child in my arms. He is so tiny. How can the weight of ages rest on his shoulders?

I hear a noise, voices, shadows, figures in the night. I bring the child closer. I am frightened. Joseph moves forward toward the entrance of the cave.

The tiny lamb snuggles close, giving warmth and comfort to my child. The shepherds speak of angels and hosannas, of seeing the glory of God. I am overwhelmed. I do not understand.

"Do not be afraid." These words I remember, words of comfort, words of hope.

These simple shepherds have been touched by God. They have been called, invited to share the story, the message, the mystery. They will never be the same.

Reflection

What message have you received? What are you called to share?

PRESENTATION IN THE TEMPLE
Luke 2:22 –38

We climbed the temple steps, Joseph and I, pausing to purchase a pair of turtledoves, an offering gift as prescribed by the law.

Several other couples were approaching the steps leading toward the temple. We nodded to each other, each couple clutching their child.

At the Mount, suddenly Simeon, a righteous man, came forward and took my child into his arms.

What a strange prayer he said. "Now, master, you may let your servant go in peace...for my eyes have seen your salvation...."

Blessing Joseph and me, he returned Jesus into my arms. His next words frightened me "...and you, yourself, a sword shall pierce." At that moment, I was reminded that as we entered the city, the cruel crosses of Roman execution greeted us. Will this be the gift offering my son will be called to make?

The priest stood at the altar. All was ready. I hesitated as he reached for my son.

I am in another space, another time. I hear the words spoken to Ahaz: "Therefore the Lord himself will give you a sign, the virgin shall be with child, and bear a son, and you shall name him Emmanuel."

My child is consecrated. My child has been offered to God.

Reflection

What in your life needs to be offered?

THE VISIT OF THE MAGI
Matthew 2:1–2, 9–11

People are still streaming into the city. The lines are long and endless. Joseph has filled out the necessary registration papers. We will rest awhile longer before we set out for home.

Some neighbors came by to visit and see the baby and wish us well.

The caravans created some questioning. Their fine royal robes and elaborate decorated camels made many curious concerning the travelers. They had come from the east, astrologers led by a star. They even sought out Herod and asked about the birth of a new-born king.

They came seeking my child. Prostrating themselves, they did him homage, these kings from the Orient. The treasures they offered (gold, frankincense, myrrh) will provide us the necessary means we need to care for him.

The sky has a new glow this evening. Stars are more numerous, and one in particular. Its tail reaches from the highest point of the sky to earth below. It is brighter than all the others. It sparkles and glimmers, reflecting the glory of God.

Reflection

What gifts do you possess? How will you put them to use?

FLIGHT TO EGYPT
Matthew 2:13 –15

It is the middle of the night. I can hardly make out
Joseph's words. What is it that he is trying to
tell me? What is all this about a dream, about
going to Egypt? We were to leave for Nazareth
in a few days.

Herod is searching for our child. That cannot be.
His intention is to destroy him! Kill him! What
does he fear? How can our child do Herod any
harm?

I do not understand. I gather our few belongings
and Joseph tends after the donkey, as we quickly
pack and leave this place.

All is quiet, not even a stirring among the trees.
Silence surrounds us. Making our way toward
the city gates, we pass a row of inns.

I press my child toward my bosom. I drape my
cloak over him. Surely the soldiers will not
stop us.

Though we have traveled this road before, so
much seems unfamiliar, foreign in the midst of
my fear.

I know safe houses abound that will welcome us,
but my questions persist.

How shall we survive? Will Joseph find work?

What awaits us in this land of Egypt?

Reflection

Fear comes in many forms. Are you fearful? What fears separate you from self, others, God?

RETURN TO NAZARETH
Matthew 23:19 –23

It is so good to be home and to be with family! The time spent in Egypt was often lonely and at times my longing for home was overwhelming.

Nazareth has grown in our absence. The well in the center of town will offer plenty of water. What a convenience not to need to go to the river bank!

It took some work putting things in order, clearing the outer room for Joseph's workshop. The table and benches for the main room are handsome and sturdy, what fine workmanship, they are large enough to fit family and friends.

Mama tells me Elizabeth and John came for a visit while Zechariah was serving in the temple. How I wish we had arrived home sooner!

Elizabeth says John speaks of a longing for the desert. His lessons at the temple have given him a desire to follow the prophets into solitude and prayer. He is a sensitive boy always thinking, studying, probing the scriptures.

We must take a trip to Judah. There is so much I want to share with Elizabeth. It will be good for Jesus and John to know one another.

Oh, there is so much yet to be done! The local school opens soon, Jesus will need to register for classes. It will be good for him to have friends to share with. There were not a great many friends in Egypt.

There will also be many chores, working with Joseph in the carpenter shop, tending after the animals, helping me in the garden. How he loves to see the seeds grow and blossom! There will also be time for play, for enjoyment, for being with classmates and friends.

Oh, how I dreamed of returning home! It is good for us to be here!

Reflection

There is an old adage that says: Home is where your heart is. Are you home?

FINDING IN THE TEMPLE
Luke 2:41 –52

How many times Joseph and I planned for this pilgrimage. How often we spoke of coming up to Jerusalem. Passover is such a time of remembrance.

The temple in Jerusalem is as no other. The magnificence of its structure. The vastness of the building. The temple guards stand at attention. Going over the threshold is as if you are taken into the very presence of the most high. It truly is a dream come true.

How good that Jesus is with us here in Jerusalem, experiencing all the ceremonies and rituals, especially now as he prepares for his bar mitzvah.

These days have been special, but we must prepare to leave, to meet the others before dawn. It is necessary to get an early start.

The men ahead calculate the miles we must cover before breaking for the night. Some are leading the wagons and donkeys, some on foot. The older women are riding. Some of us are making plans as we walk the dirt-covered road: there is much awaiting us at home. The children run alongside the road playing; some are tending to the younger ones.

Sundown is not far off. We will pitch tent soon. One more day's journey should bring us home.

Joseph came toward me; he had been with the men tending the animals. He was carrying more wood for the fire, but Jesus was not with him.

We've searched the entire camp among relatives and acquaintances. Where can he be? Was he left behind? Did Joseph think he was with me, and did I think he was with Joseph? He is lost, we must return to Jerusalem.

We have been everywhere, but still there is no sign of Jesus. Where are we to go? What are we to do? What if he's been taken? So many caravans pass this way. He surely must be hungry. What if he's been hurt? His father and I are heartbroken.

It is the third day. There seems to be some commotion, in the temple alcove. Several rabbis are sitting in a circle and a number of people surround them.

There is Jesus in the midst of the teachers, listening to them and asking them questions!

My God, I thank you that we have found him.

His answer to my question about staying in Jerusalem was strange and difficult to understand. "Did you not know that

I must be in my father's house?" Yet he looked so at home among the teachers.

Reflection

Mary and Joseph searched for Jesus, fearing that he was lost. When you seem to be lost and unable to find Jesus, where do you search for him?

THE DEATH OF JOSEPH

In the end, it was very peaceful. I held Joseph in my arms. Jesus knelt beside him, placing his head on Joseph's chest.

The love that drew us together had long existed, but at this moment each fiber of our being held this tender, sweet man as never before.

He was such a caring man, sensitive, warm, kind; always anticipating, always there with a gentle word, a knowing smile, always giving of himself.

How I will miss him! Again, my soul has been pierced. I've always been dependent on him. I remember the look in his eyes the night he spoke to my parents. That look grew more knowing, more loving, over the years we had together. His strength gave me courage, hope, joy. Nothing was too difficult: the long hours in the carpenter shop, the relentless searching for work in Egypt, his willingness to take any job, no matter how demeaning.

We would sit together for hours, sharing the events of the day or planning a special outing. The flat surface of the roof offered us a place to enjoy the cool evening breeze from the mountains, a relief from the day's heat.

We shared our ancient rituals and Sabbath customs. Joseph took delight and care in exploring the scriptures and explaining each detail of the law to Jesus. How Joseph treasured the time he spent with our son!

Jesus tried so hard to hold back his tears, but his love for Joseph was deep and lasting. He spoke of his father with affection, tenderness, and insight.

How proud I was!

Reflection

Joseph's relationship with Mary and Jesus grew and deepened as husband and father. How is your relationship with Joseph? Do you know Joseph?

A TIME OF
MINISTRY

BAPTISM OF JESUS
Matthew 3:13–17

News has reached us of John's preaching and baptizing at the Jordan. He has become the voice of one preparing the way of the Lord, as the prophets of old, who called the people to repentance and a change of heart. Elizabeth and Zachary prepared their son well.

His time has also come; Jesus leaves Nazareth in the morning. My heart is heavy, yet I know that his destiny must be fulfilled. It is for this that he has come into the world.

I wonder how he will be received. Will his message be heard?

Who will care for his needs? Where will he lay his head? Who will take him in? A mother's heart is anxious for her child.

Perhaps he and John will share their destiny together.

John and Jesus greeted one another. Their eyes met. It was as if they had been transported to another time, a day when both had leaped and danced in Elizabeth's and my wombs.

John spoke words of protest, proclaiming he was

not worthy to carry the sandals of the one who was to come.

Jesus urged John to allow him to be baptized. It was only fitting that they should share this moment together.

The sky opened and the Father declared his pleasure. "You are my beloved son; in whom I take delight."

Reflection

John recognized Jesus and pointed others in his direction. Do you point others toward Jesus?

WEDDING AT CANA
John 2:1–12

The couple were town folk. Her parents used to
visit and share in temple gatherings. Joseph once
mended a favorite chair. Later they purchased a
storage chest, perhaps for her dowry. I believe
the oldest son was in class with Jesus.

It was such a lovely ceremony. How happy and
radiant they looked! I remember how Joseph and
I drank from the cup. Everyone shouted mazel tov,
and the music began. Oh, yes! I remember!

Weddings are such joy-filled events. Everyone
has a good time and there is plenty of food
and drink, music and merriment.

For the couple it is the start of a new life together.
The beginning of putting their plans and dreams
into action. Oh, yes, I remember!

I'm so glad Jesus was able to attend. He has not
visited for some time. He looks thin. I must get
some good food into him. I hope he will stay a
day or two. These friends he's with, disciples,
seem like good men; perhaps they will take
part in his mission.

The waiter told me there is no more wine. He
didn't know what to do. He spoke to the person in

charge. This young couple and family did not need to be embarrassed.

I found Jesus and spoke to him of my concern.

The water jugs were filled to the rim. The waiters were astonished, the guests pleased, the couple filled with delight, the disciples amazed.

The new wine was of choicest quality.

Reflection

Mary sought out Jesus in a difficult situation. When problems enter your life, where do you go for solutions?

WOMAN CAUGHT IN ADULTERY
John 8:1–11

Yes, she had been with Jesus from the beginning of his ministry; for it was early on when he had looked deep into her eyes as no one else ever had. It was a piercing look and yet one of compassion, one of forgiveness, one of love. Her life would never be the same. There were always tears in her eyes when she told what had happened that afternoon.

A crowd had gathered, everyone waiting, watching, wondering what would happen. They had dragged her before him shouting accusations, ready to stone her. She needed to be made an example. After all, her reputation, or lack of it, was well known by all the townsfolk. Now they would use her to confront him.

There she stood in full view of everyone, not able to lift her head, too ashamed to make eye contact, too frightened at the consequences that awaited her. How strange that he did not speak at first, but knelt down and began writing in the dirt.

The stones fell from their hands. Slowly, silently, they walked away. Suddenly they were alone and her life was changed.

Her love for him was strong, deep, and unwavering.

Reflection

The woman's love for Jesus was born out of his unconditional love of her. He first loved her and she returned that love. Do you know Jesus' love for you?

MARY OF MAGDALA
Mark 16:9–11

Mary had long been a follower, a true friend. She knew how I worried about him, so she would send word of his whereabouts and how he was. She tended to his needs and shocked everyone by anointing his head and wiping her tears from his feet with her hair.

She had been driven by demons, seven of them. She had no peace. Possessed, she became their prisoner. She struggled and thrashed herself about seeking freedom from the chains that bound her.

This woman from Magdala and Jesus faced each other, and at that moment the demons left her. She stood at my side beneath his cross watching him die. She gave me comfort and strength. Together we anointed his body and wept as they placed him in the tomb.

That morning was like no other. Her heart was broken. She could hardly catch her breath running the entire distance from the tomb. "They have taken him, the stone is rolled away, he is gone!" Peter and John returned with her to verify what she was saying. Indeed, he was not there. Staying on at the tomb weeping, she heard her name "Mary," as she had never heard before. Recognizing him, she fell to her knees.

Mary was the disciple of the Resurrection! She was sent to announce to the others that he lives! She was a dear companion after his leave-taking. I enjoyed our heart-to-heart conversations.

Reflection

Jesus told Mary not to cling to him, but to announce his resurrection to the brethren. How do you proclaim that Jesus lives? Do you announce his resurrection?

ZACCHAEUS
Luke 19:1 –10

Zacchaeus was a little man, a tax collector, hated by the people for conspiring with the Roman authorities. He was well dressed, lived comfortably, had several servants.

He looked so foolish sitting up there in the middle of the tree. The crowd laughed at him and shouted, while children kept pointing up at him. Dogs barked and tried to climb up to where he was perched.

Suddenly a silence came over the crowd. There was Jesus looking up and telling Zacchaeus that he would dine with him that evening.

Of all the people along the route that day, why would Jesus choose him? It was only as they sat sharing food, lost in conversation that Zacchaeus found the reason.

That night salvation had been given and accepted, and a friendship began.

Reflection

Zacchaeus' encounter with Jesus changed his life. Is your life in need of change? Have you encountered Jesus?

THE FEEDING OF THE
FIVE THOUSAND
Mark 6:34 –44

I had come to Capernaum. It was late afternoon.
A large crowd had gathered, hoping he would
arrive. They had been there all day.

A boat was approaching. As the men pulled it into
the shore line, Jesus disembarked. There was great
excitement. The crowd was vast, so many in need
of healing, in need of being touched, in need of
being led. They were as sheep without a
shepherd.

The disciples were extremely upset, the more they
tried to disburse the crowd, the more people ran
toward them. I was afraid the crowd would
overtake him.

A young boy came forward with a few loaves and
some fish. The disciples had the people sit in
small groups on the grassy hillside.

Taking what the boy offered, Jesus blessed the
fish, broke the bread, and set it before the people.
He knew of their hunger.

When all had been satisfied, twelve baskets of
fragments were collected.

Reflection

Jesus knows what you hunger for. Ask him to feed you!

THE REJECTION
AT NAZARETH
Matthew 13:54–58

He had been traveling all across Galilee and Samaria. The crowds were always there. He hardly had time for any rest. There were the sick and poor, the blind and lame, those possessed of evil spirits. So many were seeking healing, seeking forgiveness.

He came home to visit. I fed him his favorite meals. We spoke long into the night. We walked the familiar hillside, and enjoyed remembering... times when he had run playfully along these same roads...the time he and Joseph surprised me with a new wooden chest. It was good to have him home.

It was early morning. We walked together toward the synagogue. Friends and neighbors greeted us along the way. He picked up the scriptures and began to teach. Life-long friends and neighbors became astonished, their faces angry. His words fell on closed ears and hardened hearts. They took offense at him. Jesus sadly said to them, "A prophet is not without honor except in his native place and in his own house." We turned and walked out of the synagogue.

He quietly left that afternoon.

Reflection

At times familiarity breeds contempt and jealousy. Do I need to look at those who are familiar to me through different eyes?

CLEANSING OF
THE TEMPLE
Matthew 21:12–17

It was like any other day. He had been among the
people teaching, listening, curing their sick.

He came upon the temple area and entered, not
expecting to see what he found. Confusion
abounded. The lines were long and disorderly.
The money changers allowed by Herod abused
the rights of the people, levying extra fees. Those
selling animals for sacrifice had increased prices.
People were shouting and becoming agitated.

As he moved into the area, he began to turn over
the tables and drive out those engaged in selling
and buying. One table after another came
bounding to the floor. Sheep ran in every
direction, people fled, the disciples watched in
amazement. Never before had they seen his
anger and frustration so vividly shown.

His words rang out echoing off the temple walls,
"My Father's house shall be a house of prayer,
but you are making it a den of thieves."

The chief priests and scribes were indignant that
Jesus healed the blind and the lame and did not
quiet the children crying, "Hosanna to the Son
of David."

I feared for his safety amidst all the chaos and disorder!

Reflection

The temple was a sacred place, a place to communicate with God. Where is that sacred place for you to converse with your God?

THE RAISING OF LAZARUS
John 11:1–44

Bethany had become a home away from home. Lazarus, Mary, and Martha had opened their home to him. He would find solace and rest there. He enjoyed their companionship, and was free to be himself. I, too, was welcomed and spent many delightful visits in their home.

Martha was a superb cook. The aroma from her kitchen would make your mouth water with anticipation. Mary was attentive to Jesus and treasured the long conversations they shared together. Lazarus was well known; he had a thriving business and was highly respected. They were family to us.

The news of Lazarus' illness was startling and unexpected. I left immediately to be with Mary and Martha. When I arrived at Bethany, Lazarus was already dead. We were all distraught and unable to understand what was keeping Jesus. Word had been sent to him, and the hope was that he would arrive and save Lazarus.

He was not at a distance. After all, he had cured so many others. Surely he could command the illness to depart.

Martha ran out to the edge of town when word arrived that he was near. Mary and I, together with those who had come to offer their comfort, followed. As we embraced one another, Martha voiced her sorrow and request. Mary and I looked deeply into his eyes, which were filled with tears. He began to weep bitterly, for his love of Lazarus was great.

Jesus spoke of resurrection and new life. When we approached the tomb, he ordered the stone to be taken away. All who heard were amazed. Martha questioned the stench. Lazarus had been buried four days.

Raising his eyes toward heaven, Jesus cried out "Lazarus, come out!" Lazarus, tied hand and foot with burial bands, his face wrapped in a cloth, came out and stood before us. "Untie him."

The rejoicing began for Lazarus was again in our midst!

Reflection

The raising of Lazarus glorified God. What do you need to do to give glory to God?

A TIME OF
SORROW

JESUS' TRIUMPHANT ENTRY
INTO JERUSALEM
John 12:12 –19

My heart is troubled. Jesus tells me his eyes are set
on Jerusalem. My thoughts go back to another
time when I had thought we had lost him. Oh,
the pain his father and I felt! That feeling of loss
overwhelms me again. Jerusalem is not safe for
him. Once again Simeon's words ring in my
ears: "This child is destined to cause the
fall and rise of many in Israel and a sword
will pierce your own soul."

The crowds are swelling. The market place is
filled. Passover is but a few days away and the
shoppers are hurriedly buying their provisions.

The voices and shouts became louder and more
clear: "Hosanna in the highest; blessed is he
who comes in the name of the Lord!"

I got a glimpse of him seated on a donkey. It was
as if the whole city cried out in one voice. The
palm branches swayed against the sky. The
enthusiasm and energy of the crowd overtook
the soldiers. They simply stepped aside as he
entered the city.

Perhaps this time it will be different. Finally
they see him for who he is. And yet my heart is
heavy.

Reflection

Mary's heart is filled with joy as the crowd proclaims her son to be the one who comes in the name of the Lord. Finally they have come to know who he is.

Who is Jesus for you?

THE PASSOVER MEAL
John 13:1-17

The Passover feast will soon be celebrated. Jesus
has sent Peter and John to make all the necessary
preparations for the seder meal. I must gather the
other women. We will all meet at the upper room.

The market place will be crowded. No doubt
visitors are already arriving and the vendors will
be out to sell their wares. Peter and John will need
to arrive early in order to select the best and
bargain for the prices.

Dinner is ready. The lamb was a good size, young
and unblemished.

How sacred this time of remembering! The bitter
herbs tell the story of ancient bondage in a foreign
land and of Yahweh's gentle care for his people.

I, too, remember a foreign land far from home.
This meal was as no other. The old rituals remain.
Yet whatever made him begin to wash
our feet! He says he has given an example to
be followed.

Peter certainly put up a fuss, as Jesus approached
him to wash his feet. When he had finished, Jesus
sat at the table and said:

"Take eat, this is my body. Take drink, this is my
blood. Do this to remember me."

Could this be what these years of teaching, these years of wandering the countryside, these years of ministry, have been about?

Is his time near? Once again his words of long ago ring in my ears: "I must be about my father's business."

Reflection

Jesus says he has given an example. Whose feet do you need to wash? Who has washed your feet? Jesus was about his father's business. Whose business are you about?

JESUS SENTENCED TO BE CRUCIFIED
John 19:1–36

I can hardly get through the crowd. John came as quickly as he could with the news that they had taken Jesus to Pilate.

What could be the purpose? Why would he be dragged away, taken prisoner? He is no criminal.

Surely this broken figure of a man could not be my son? His body was an open sore. The lashes had torn open his flesh. The hideous crown of disgrace pierces his brow. The blood and sweat that covered his face made him look less than human.

The shouts from the crowd terrified me. The cries of hosanna had turned ugly. The words of execution from the chief priests and guards ring in my ears: "Crucify him, crucify him."

The soldiers placed the heavy cross upon his shoulders. The weight caused him to stumble. I needed to get through the crowd. If only I could touch him.

One of the soldiers let me by and for one brief moment our eyes meet. My thoughts were drawn back to when Joseph first placed him into my arms. Was it not just yesterday? Where have the years gone? How could Simon have known his destiny and mine?

Surely he would die before we reached Golgotha. He had fallen again and again. Even with Simon's help, each step became slower, more painful. His agony could not continue much longer.

The pounding rang in my ears. The friction of the hammer against the nails pierced my whole being. He hung between heaven and earth, my son, stripped of all human appearance.

His sentence written for all to read: Jesus of Nazareth, the king of the Jews. If only they knew. If only they had recognized the fulfillment of the scriptures and how true this proclamation was.

His torment was heightened by the insults of the crowd. My God! My God! Have mercy! Have pity on my son!

The weakness that overtook me is but a shadow of his. The tears I weep are for all mothers who bear the death of a child. The loss of a child.

He is flesh of my flesh. The blood that flowed from him is mine. The life that slowly left his body lived within my womb.

He began to speak: "Here is your son; here is your mother." Dear John, I am now his and the world's.

The sky became dark. The wind swept across the hillside. The silence was pierced by his cry: "It is finished."

My son bowed his head and gave up his spirit.

Reflection

Mary walked the road to Calvary with her son. How willing are you to take the same road? Mary watches her son give completely, even his life out of love. What are you being asked to give out of love?

THE BURIAL OF JESUS
John 19:38 –42

Joseph and Nicodemus have returned. They have convinced Pilate to give us the body. Slowly they lifted him off the cross and placed him into my arms. My dead son. I held him close to me.

His eyes are shut. The deep, loving glance that twinkled and made his eyes dance is no more.

His hair is knotted with twigs from the crown, mixed with blood.

I wash his face. The spit, sweat, and blood are hardened and caked. I remember bathing him as a child. How he splashed and relished the water. How dear those tender moments were!

I pour the mixture of spices and aloes into the open wounds. I remember the myrrh of long ago, when the Magi presented their gifts and offered homage.

Martha and Mary of Magdala help me bind Jesus with the customary burial cloth. Sundown is approaching and we must hurry.

There is a new tomb in the nearby garden. They will lay him there.

I struggle to release him. I want so much to hold him, to keep him with me. How does a mother give up her child? What anguish can be compared to this?

He is carried to the tomb. The stone is rolled across the entrance. I am alone. No longer a wife! No longer a mother!

"I am the resurrection and the life, whoever believes in me, even if he dies will live." Were these not his words?

Yes! I do believe!

Reflection

Mary's heart is broken. Her son is rejected. Yet she remains faith-filled. When rejection and brokenness surround you, in whom, and where, do you place your faith?

A TIME OF
G L O R Y

THE EMPTY TOMB/THE RESURRECTION
John 20:1–10

It's early morning the third day. The women are planning to go to the tomb.

John forced me to rest, but sleep would not come. My thoughts wandered to times and places long past, Bethlehem, Egypt, Nazareth. The night lay heavy. The hours seemed endless.

I remember happier days. Joseph's skillful hands carving and molding shapes into chairs, cradles, chests, tables, sturdy handsome pieces that would last a lifetime. Jesus was at his side handing him tools, and Joseph was teaching him the art he so loved. Oh, how I long for Joseph to be at my side!

The events of these days were spoken of in the words of the prophets, words I have kept within my heart, knowing that my child, my son, was to fulfill the promise of long ago.

Can this be the means? Can shame and suffering, pain and death bring new life?

Peoples' hearts can be so cold at times. He called them a stiff-neck people. Didn't he make the blind to see and the lame to walk? Didn't he calm the sea? Did he not make the paralytic skip down the road? Did he not feed them with a few loaves and a couple of fish? What of Lazarus? Even the religious leaders were present as they untied the wrappings that bound him. This cannot be. I hear a greeting. Mother/Mama! It is Jesus, my son? He lives!

It is not the end! It is the beginning!

Reflection

Mary trusted and believed. Be in touch with the mystery of life, death, and new life...life everlasting. Be open to new birth.

THE ROAD TO EMMAUS
Luke 24:13 –35

There was pounding at the door. Peter hesitated to answer. So much had taken place in a short period of time. The soldiers were canvassing the area. Shutters were closed and doors locked. No one was on the street.

The two were exhausted, out of breath. They had ran all the way from Emmaus, miles away.

They could hardly contain themselves. Before one was finished speaking, the other began. They were ecstatic; their words were filled with exhilaration and joy.

A new understanding of the scriptures had been given to them. They recognized Jesus in the breaking of the bread. All their expectations, all their dreams, had been fulfilled. The one who was to redeem Israel had come!

He truly lives!

Reflection

Who are those with whom you break bread? Do you recognize Jesus?

THE ASCENSION
Acts 1:6-12

There has been such joy among his followers:
Magdalene's delight at seeing him. Peter's
swimming to shore from the boat after John
recognized that it was Jesus, the breakfast he
prepared for the disciples, Thomas's declaration.
Jesus' gentle greeting: "Peace be with you." Peter's
being commissioned and given the name "Rock."

So many had become distraught, had not
understood the ancient prophecy, were
discouraged, and gave into feelings of doubt.

Now the joy within our hearts can not be taken
from us, for he lives and the prophecy is
completed.

The Father's words have been fulfilled "You are
my beloved Son; with you I am well pleased."

His words burn within our hearts "Go, make
disciples....Baptize them...teach them to observe
what I have commanded....I am with you
always."

Jesus came last evening. We talked long into the
night of times past, of joys, sorrows, of Joseph,
of all that had come to pass.

I want so much to be with him. To hold onto him,
but I know he must return to the Father. He says I

must remain for a while longer. As they begin their missionary journeys, the disciples will need my encouragement, my strength, my words, my prayers.

This time, however, I will not lose him. We will be together soon.

Reflection

Mary knew that Jesus' farewell would bring about new hellos. Are you a person of farewells? Or hellos?

PENTECOST
Acts 2:1-13

This place, this room, brings me back to our last supper together, when he began to wash our feet and speak of a new commandment.

This space has become our refuge since his return to the Father. It still is not safe to walk the streets. The temple guards are daily bringing followers before the religious leaders.

Many are coming to us under cover of darkness. We share stories, sing hymns, read the scriptures, and gather together for the breaking of the bread.

John has been so attentive to my needs. On evenings when we come together, he and the others ask me to tell the stories of Bethlehem, Egypt, of Joseph and Jesus and our life together in Nazareth.

It is early. The sun has just begun to climb over the horizon. The morning air is fresh and clean.

Peter and the others come up the steps and enter. The women have prepared a simple breakfast.

Suddenly, without any warning the wind filled the entire house. The strength of its force overcame us. It was as if the floor was not beneath our feet.

Tongues of fire came to rest over each of us. The energy grew until the advocate took possession of our entire being. Jesus' promise has been kept. We were baptized in the Holy Spirit.

Reflection

Have you been baptized in the Holy Spirit? Does the knowledge of being baptized in the Spirit fill you with energy and with the desire for God in your life?

LIFE IN THE CHRISTIAN COMMUNITY
Acts 2:42 –47, 3:1 –10

…"Thou are Peter and upon this rock I will build my Church…."How these words must ring in Peter's ears. Yes, he has taken on the role of leader. His words are bold and challenging. All look to him for guidance.

The crowds were filled with amazement as Peter took the beggar by the hand and lifted him to his feet.

He and the others became witnesses to my son's mission.

They preach each day in the temple area and we share together in the breaking of the bread. Our voices are one in prayer and thanksgiving to Yahweh.

Each day the number of followers continues to grow. There is a common purse and all is shared according to one's needs.

I understand now why I needed to remain behind. They come to me for encouragement and in our storytelling we find strength and faith. I must help them to keep focused. Jesus must be their cornerstone, their center, as we form community together.

His reign has begun!

Reflection

Mary's role in the Church is inseparable from her union with her son. Through her prayers she aided the beginnings of the Church, invoking the Spirit to rest upon it. Mary becomes the Church's model of faith and charity.

What is Church for you? What role do you play?

Epilog

Mary, teenager with child,
wife and partner,
refugee in a foreign land,
friend and companion,
first disciple,
model of the church,
committed and faithful,
your journey of new beginnings
and ministry, of sorrow and glory bids
us to pray "Hail, Holy Queen."

MARY, QUEEN OF HEAVEN AND EARTH

Mary, you are a woman, flesh of our flesh. You know the beat of a woman's heart, a woman's sensitivity, a woman's desire for relationship and love. You know a woman's fear and suffering, a woman's disappointment and loneliness.

You know what it means to be a teenager with child, confused, afraid and shunned.

You know what it means to be a mother, aching for the needs of her child: shelter, food, understanding, and welcoming.

You know the fear of a mother for her child, that harm and violence will overtake her child.

You know the struggle to let children go, the worry and concern for the road they take; the desire to hold them in, to protect them, to provide so all their dreams can be accomplished.

You know a love that only a mother can know, an abiding nurturing love, a love that sacrifices life itself, a love that beats in another's heart, a love that births life and flesh and blood.

You know a love of new encounters, new greetings, new adventures, new relationships, a love of friendships, companionships, a love of sisterhood and brotherhood, a love of humanity for humanity.

You know a gentle love, you know a tender love, you know a heartfelt love, you know an embracing love.

You know the life of a refugee, a woman in a foreign land, among strangers, with different customs, speaking a different tongue, possessing different traditions, far from family and friends, losing what is familiar, comfortable.

You know the loss of a partner, a soulmate, a beloved, the loneliness of a widow, of the one that is left behind.

But you also know a love that is faithful, trusting, supportive, a love of family and relatives, of husband and friend, a love that conquers all narrowness of mind, a love that nourishes and deepens, a love that is life-giving.

A love that says: "Well done, my faithful daughter!" "Welcome home, Mother!"